Belongs To

Made in United States
Orlando, FL
30 November 2024

54720247R00055